SIAMESE Cats

by Joanne Mattern

CAPSTONE PRESS
a capstone imprint

Edge Books are published by Capstone Press,
1710 Roe Crest Drive, North Mankato, Minnesota 56003.
www.capstonepub.com

Books published by Capstone Press are manufactured with paper
containing at least 10 percent post-consumer waste.

Library of Congress Cataloging-in-Publication Data
Mattern, Joanne, 1963–
    Siamese cats / by Joanne Mattern.
    p. cm.—(Edge books. All about cats)
  Includes bibliographical references and index.
  Summary: "Describes the history, physical features, temperament, and care of
    the Siamese cat breed"—Provided by publisher.
  ISBN 978-1-4296-6635-0 (library binding)
  1. Siamese cat—Juvenile literature. I. Title.
  SF449.S5M38 2011
  636.8'25—dc22   2010033720

Editorial Credits
Connie R. Colwell and Carrie Braulick Sheely, editors; Heidi Thompson,
    designer; Wanda Winch, media researcher; Eric Manske,
    production specialist

Photo Credits
Alamy: blickwinkel, 12, Juniors Bildarchiv, cover, 16; Photo by Fiona Green, 5, 7,
    21, 23, 25, 26, 28; Shutterstock: Aleisha Evans, 15 (inset), Charlie Edward, 9,
    Ekaterina Cherkashina, 11, Konstantin_K, 17, Linn Currie, 19, MAErtek, 15

Printed in the United States of America in Stevens Point, Wisconsin.
122011   006527WZVMI

TABLE OF CONTENTS

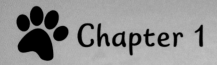

Chapter 1

A FAMOUS BREED

Ask your friends to name a few cat breeds. Chances are that the Siamese will be included in their responses. Siamese cats are one of the best-known cat breeds in the world. People enjoy the Siamese for many reasons. Siamese are friendly, intelligent, and attractive cats that make excellent pets.

The Siamese breed has even received some attention in movies. In the 1950s, Peggy Lee and Sonny Burke wrote "The Siamese Cat Song" for the Disney company. Disney used it in the movie *Lady and the Tramp*.

In 2009 the Siamese was the fourth most popular breed in the Cat Fanciers' Association (CFA). It was the second most popular shorthair breed. The CFA is the world's largest cat **registry**.

The Siamese probably gets much of its popularity from its one-of-a-kind look. These cats have bold **colorpoints** and slanted blue eyes. A very slender, yet athletic body also sets them apart from other breeds.

registry—an organization that keeps track of the ancestry for cats of a certain breed

colorpoint—a pattern in which the ears, face, tail, and feet are darker than the base color

FACT: Siamese cats are very vocal. They are known for making a raspy yowl.

The colorpoints of the Siamese attract many people to the breed.

IS THE SIAMESE RIGHT FOR YOU?

Siamese cats have friendly personalities. They seem to enjoy being around people and other animals. Siamese often make good pets for families with children, dogs, or other cats.

Siamese do not do well alone. They often seem unhappy without people or other animals to spend time with. Siamese owners who are not at home for long periods of time may want to adopt another cat. The two cats will be company for each other while the owners are away.

Few health problems are associated with the Siamese breed. Siamese are also easy to care for. Their short coats need very little grooming.

FINDING A SIAMESE

You can find a Siamese cat in several ways. The best way to find a Siamese kitten is by visiting a breeder. Most breeders take steps to be sure the cats they sell are healthy. You can also adopt a Siamese through a breed rescue organization or an animal shelter. These organizations help find new homes for pets. Cats from a breed rescue organization may even be registered.

Owning more than one cat will help keep your Siamese from becoming bored.

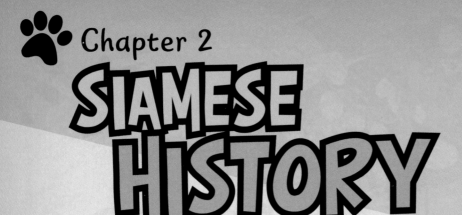

Chapter 2

SIAMESE HISTORY

The Siamese breed has a long history. People do not know exactly where the Siamese breed began. Siamese cats get their name from the eastern Asian region of Siam. Today this country is known as Thailand.

In the 1500s, Siamese cats were sacred to the Siamese people. People believed that owning these cats brought good luck. Siamese cats may have lived as pets in Buddhist temples. People think the cats might have warned Buddhist priests of strangers. The cats also may have lived with the king of Siam.

LEGEND FROM THE PAST

Siamese cats of the past often had kinked tails and crossed eyes. These features no longer are common in the breed. But one of the most popular legends about Siamese cats describes how they got these features. According to the legend, two Siamese cats named Tien and Chula lived with a monk in a Buddhist temple. The monk was in charge of guarding a sacred cup.

Past members of Thailand's royalty built some of the country's most majestic temples. Siamese cats might have led plush lives in these huge buildings.

One day the monk disappeared, and Tien left to search for a new monk. Chula stayed in the temple to guard the cup. Chula watched the cup for many days and began to grow tired. She decided to hook her tail around the cup so she could sleep. She knew that no one could take the cup from under her tail without waking her.

Finally, Tien returned with a new monk. Chula was still guarding the cup. But Chula's eyes were crossed from watching the cup for so long. Her tail was kinked from holding the cup. She also had given birth to kittens. The kittens had crossed eyes and kinked tails like Chula.

CATS OF ROYALTY

The legend of Chula and Tien is a made-up story. But there is no doubt that the Siamese has royalty in its roots. Siamese cats were important members of Siam's royal court. A Siamese cat was placed in the tomb of each dead king. Workers dug a hole in each tomb so the cat could escape.

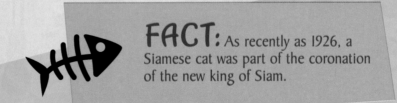

FACT: As recently as 1926, a Siamese cat was part of the coronation of the new king of Siam.

When the cat came out, people believed the king's soul was inside the cat. The sacred cat then became part of the royal court. Its job was to watch over the new king. When the cat died, people believed it carried the dead king's soul into the afterlife.

A few Siamese still are born with crossed eyes.

Since the early 1900s, Siamese have been popular at cat shows around the world.

POPULARITY SPREADS AROUND THE WORLD

Officials from the British government came to Siam in the late 1800s. They had never seen a cat like the Siamese. Many British travelers brought Siamese cats home with them. At first many Europeans thought these cats were strange and ugly. But some people wanted to own the unusual cats.

In 1884 the king of Siam gave two Siamese cats named Pho and Mia to a British official. The cats became popular in Great Britain. In 1885 Pho and Mia had kittens. The kittens won prizes at the 1885 Crystal Palace cat show in London.

Siamese cats also made their way into the hearts of Americans in the late 1800s. In 1878 Rutherford B. Hayes was the U.S. president. Hayes' wife received a Siamese cat named Siam as a gift. The cat became sick and died a few months later. But Siam helped create interest in the breed. By the early 1900s, Siamese cats were appearing in U.S. cat shows.

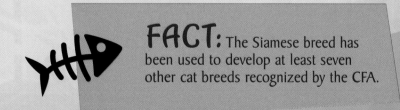

FACT: The Siamese breed has been used to develop at least seven other cat breeds recognized by the CFA.

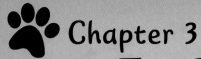

Chapter 3

COLOR-POINTED AND CLASSY

Today most Siamese cats look different from those of the past. In the past, Siamese had round heads. But modern Siamese have triangular, wedge-shaped heads. Today's Siamese also have larger ears and longer, more slender bodies than Siamese of the past. The CFA and some other registries allow only Siamese with this modern appearance in cat shows.

COLORS

The four original colors of Siamese cats are called classic Siamese colors. These colors occur naturally in the breed. They include seal point, chocolate point, blue point, and lilac point. The seal-point color is the best known. Seal-point cats have light coats with dark brown points. On some cats, the dark brown shade almost appears black. On a chocolate-point Siamese, the points are a lighter brown. The blue color looks like a shade of gray. Blue-point cats have blue-white bodies with blue points. Lilac-point Siamese have pink-gray points with white bodies.

FACT: Some people still breed Siamese cats with round heads and sturdy bodies. These cats are called traditional or applehead Siamese.

traditional Siamese

The CFA officially recognized the blue-point Siamese in 1934.

15

Over time people have mated Siamese with other breeds. This breeding has produced **hybrid** Siamese with a variety of coat colors. These colors include tabby point and red point. Tabby-point Siamese have faintly striped coats and heavily striped points. Red-point Siamese have light bodies and red points.

The CFA allows only Siamese with classic colors to be shown. It considers Siamese without classic colors to be a separate breed called the Colorpoint Shorthair. Some other registries allow Siamese of all colors to be shown.

On a red-point Siamese, the shade of red can vary from faint to a dark orange-red color.

hybrid—the offspring of two different breeds

16

WHAT CAUSES COLORPOINTS?

A special gene in Siamese cats causes them to have colorpoints. This gene is heat-sensitive. Cool parts of the Siamese body have dark fur. Warm parts have light fur. All animals with this gene are born with white coats. The cooler parts of Siamese kittens' bodies turn dark when they are between 4 months and 1 year old. Fur on other parts of the body also may turn darker as the cat grows older.

BODIES

Siamese are medium-sized cats. Males are often larger than females. Males usually weigh between 8 and 10 pounds (3.6 and 4.5 kilograms). The average weight of females is between 5 and 7 pounds (2.3 and 3.2 kg).

Modern Siamese have long, slender bodies that give them an elegant look. The hips are about the same width as the shoulders. Even though the cats are slender, they have firm muscles. Long, slim legs match the cats' tubular bodies. A thin, tapered tail completes the graceful look of the Siamese.

Siamese have very short coats. The hair lies close to the body and has a glossy appearance.

FACIAL FEATURES

The face of the modern Siamese is a big part of its unique look. Modern Siamese have wedge-shaped heads. The wedge starts at the nose and flares outward. The large ears of a Siamese are wide at the base and pointed at the tips.

All Siamese have blue eyes. The eyes are almond-shaped and slanted toward the nose.

tapered—to be more narrow at one end than the other

PERSONALITY

Siamese are known for being social and loyal. They meow loudly to people as if they are talking to them. Siamese often bond closely with one person.

Siamese cats are also playful and intelligent. They seem to like games such as chasing and fetching balls. Some Siamese can be trained to do tricks or walk on a leash.

Siamese have athletic bodies that help them jump high.

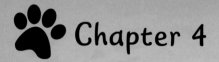

Chapter 4

CARING FOR A SIAMESE

Siamese are strong, healthy cats. With good care, they can live 15 years or more.

Like all cats, Siamese should be kept indoors. Cats that are allowed to roam outside face dangers from cars and other animals. They are also more likely to develop diseases.

FEEDING

Siamese cats need a balanced, healthy diet. You can find high-quality cat foods at pet stores or supermarkets.

You can choose to feed your Siamese dry food or moist food. Dry food helps keep cats' teeth clean. Since it won't spoil, you can leave a day's worth of dry food in the cat's dish. Moist food will spoil. It shouldn't be left out for more than one hour.

The amount of food needed depends on the individual cat. Use the instructions on your pet food package as a guideline.

Cats need plenty of water to stay healthy. Owners should always keep their cats' bowls filled with fresh, clean water.

Some owners leave out a set amount of food for their cats each day.

LITTER BOXES

Your Siamese will need a litter box. Cats get rid of bodily waste in litter boxes. Be sure to keep the litter box clean. Remove waste from the box each day. Change the litter about every two weeks or when the litter appears lumpy or wet. Cats may refuse to use a dirty litter box.

SCRATCHING POSTS

Scratching is a natural behavior for cats. Cats mark their territories by leaving their scent on objects they scratch. Cats also scratch to release tension and keep their claws sharp. A scratching post can keep your cat from scratching on furniture and carpet.

FACT: Some cats refuse to use a litter box if it is too close to the food dish. Place the litter box in a separate area from the food dish.

litter—small bits of clay or other material used to absorb the waste of cats and other animals

A litter box should give your cat enough room to turn around.

COAT GROOMING

Siamese have sleek coats that need little care. Only occasional brushing is needed to remove loose hair. Too much brushing can damage a Siamese's coat. Some owners rub their cats' coats with a damp, soft cloth to keep the coats shiny. You can also dampen your hands and run them backward through the cat's coat.

DENTAL CARE

Siamese cats need regular dental care to remove **plaque** from their teeth and gums. Plaque can cause tooth decay and gum disease. You should brush your cat's teeth at least once each week. Use a toothbrush made for cats or a soft cloth. Always use toothpaste made for cats. Toothpaste made for people can make cats sick.

FACT: Owners who show their Siamese often trim the hair inside the cats' ears. The trimming is done to make the ears appear larger.

plaque—the coating of food, saliva, and bacteria that forms on teeth and can cause tooth decay

Occasional brushing will help keep your Siamese's coat shiny and sleek.

A nail trimmer made for cats can help
reduce the risk of injury to your cat.

NAIL CARE

Like all cats, Siamese need their nails trimmed every few weeks. Trimming reduces damage if cats scratch the carpet or furniture. It also helps keep cats from getting ingrown nails. Ingrown claws can become infected.

You should start trimming a cat's nails when it is a kitten. The kitten will then become used to having its nails trimmed as it grows older.

Some people take their cats to the veterinarian to be declawed. These permanent surgeries either remove part of the claw or keep a cat from **retracting** the claw. But there are several disadvantages of declawing. Declawed cats are less able to hunt and defend themselves if they accidentally get outdoors. Declawing also can cause cats pain. For these reasons, the CFA and other organizations disapprove of declawing. Some veterinarians even refuse to declaw cats.

retract—to draw back in; cats can extend and retract their claws

HEALTH CARE

You should bring your cat to the veterinarian at least once each year. At these visits, your cat will receive any necessary **vaccinations**. The vet will also look for signs of health problems. No specific health problems are linked to the Siamese breed. Some are born with crossed eyes or kinked tails, but these features don't affect a cat's health.

Veterinarians check a cat's ears, eyes, mouth, and coat for signs of health problems at checkups.

FACT: Siamese with kinked tails are not allowed to compete in CFA shows.

If you don't plan to breed your Siamese, you should have it spayed or neutered. These surgeries keep cats from having unwanted kittens. Controlling the pet population increases the chances that pets already needing homes will be adopted. Spaying and neutering also helps keep a cat from getting certain diseases. Cats that are spayed or neutered usually have calmer personalities than cats that are not spayed or neutered.

The rewards of owning a member of the intelligent, playful Siamese breed are many. By giving your Siamese good care, you'll be able to experience these rewards year after year.

vaccination—a shot of medicine that protects animals from a disease

GLOSSARY

breed (BREED)—a certain kind of animal within an animal group; breed also means to mate and raise a certain kind of animal

colorpoint (KUHL-ur-point)—a pattern in which the ears, face, tail, and feet are darker than the base color

hybrid (HYE-brid)—the offspring of two different breeds

litter (LIT-ur)—small bits of clay or other material used to absorb the waste of cats and other animals

monk (MUHNGK)—a man who lives in a religious community and promises to devote his life to his religion

plaque (PLAK)—the coating of food, saliva, and bacteria that forms on teeth and can cause tooth decay

registry (REH-juh-stree)—an organization that keeps track of the ancestry for cats of a certain breed

retract (ree-TRAKT)—to draw back in

sacred (SAY-krid)—holy or having to do with religion

tabby (TAB-ee)—having a striped coat

tapered (TAY-purd)—to be more narrow at one end than the other

vaccination (vak-suh-NAY-shun)—a shot of medicine that protects animals from a disease

READ MORE

Hanson, Anders. *Sleek Siamese.* Cat Craze. Edina, Minn.: ABDO Pub. Co., 2010.

Stone, Lynn M. *Siamese Cats.* Eye to Eye With Cats. Vero Beach, Fla.: Rourke Publishing, 2010.

White, Nancy. *Siamese: Talk to Me!* Cat-ographies. New York: Bearport, 2011.

INTERNET SITES

FactHound offers a safe, fun way to find Internet sites related to this book. All of the sites on FactHound have been researched by our staff.

Here's all you do:

Visit *www.facthound.com*

Type in this code: 9781429666350

INDEX